In Prai
Love Can't Wait

Beautiful. I thoroughly enjoyed breathing in all these poems. There is so much truth and wisdom in Muskie's words. Such playful tenderness, too, like little lights illuminating from the page.

Seed Biggar
Songhees Territory, Victoria, BC, Canada

Muskie's poems explore themes of love, loss, Divine Presence and inner guidance. They are shining with insight and deep feeling.

Mindy Toomay, Co-Author
The Writer's Path: A Guidebook for Your Creative Journey and of a dozen books on food and cooking.

Muskie's poems speak in a touching voice. They evoke the joy and sadness, confusion and clear seeing which is our human condition. Most of all they speak to the importance of kindness and compassion.

Bob Rosenbaum, Author
Zen and the Heart of Psychotherapy and Walking the Way: 81 Zen Encounters with the Tao Te Ching

Love Can't Wait

Lve Can't Wait

Muskie Fields

Stream of Wisdom Press
San Francisco

Library of Congress Cataloguing-In-Publication Data

Names: Muskie Fields, Author
Title: Love can't wait / Muskie Fields.
Description: 1st edition. | San Francisco, CA : Stream of Wisdom Press, 2017.
Identifiers: LCCN 2017931528 | ISBN 9780998614588 (softcover)
Subjects: LCSH: Spirituality--Poetry. | Wisdom--Poetry. | Nature-- Poetry. | Buddhism--Poetry. | Sufi poetry, American. | Christian poetry. | GSAFD: Love poetry.

Classification: LCCN 2017931528 | DDC 811/.6--dc23
https:// lccn.loc.gov/2017931528

Softcover ISBN 978-0-9986145-8-8

10 9 8 7 6 5 4 3 2 1

First edition, February 2017

Printed in the United States of America

MUSKIE FIELDS

To love,
inspiration,
& the muse:

" ..there is a field, I'll meet you there."[1]

-Rumi

To the ones who will occupy
their own hearts
Who by developing their true natures and
courage will save themselves all beings &
To the the ones who will choose love over fear,
love over hate:

It is through you, the world will change.

"Just Do It."[2]

To those who do not yet know love:

"Never give up."[3]

Go forth finding the keys to all your love and
determination.

To all beings of the whole world, no one left out,
to you this book is dedicated.

[1] Rūmī, Jalāl Al-Dīn, John Moyne, and Coleman
Barks. *Open Secret: Versions of Rumi*. Putney, VT:
Threshold, 1984.
[2] Zen Master Seung Sahn. A main teaching phrase,
1972-2004.
[3] His Holiness the 14th Dalai Lama.

MUSKIE FIELDS

CONTENTS

MUSKIE FIELDS

FOREWORD

In the spirit of the mystical poets like Rumi, Muskie invites us to explore love in close human relationships and widens the inquiry to discover the truth of interconnectedness with all beings.

A quick, open gaze of a deer pierces the heart, and if you accept her invitation to read with open breath-mind, it may pierce yours too. You may find yourself viewing your own life and relationships with fresh discovery.

Later in the journey, Muskie finds deep compassion crucial in our larger social and political engagement.

"A secret garden to behold" to read with "don't know" mind.

Britton "Daigen" Pyland
Longtime Zen Student in the
Soto tradition of Suzuki Roshi

29 November 2016

MUSKIE FIELDS

ACKNOWLEDGMENTS

To my readers: Mindy Toomay, Seed Biggar of Canada. To Bob Rosenbaum & Jeanne, Guinevere & Amitabha, couples from the San Francisco Bay Area: What uncanny synchronistic meetings on the very same afternoon in two distinct locations in the town of Mount Shasta. To John Benning, Daigen Britton Pyland and to many other friends, I am grateful.

To my teachers for whom I have great affection, an order is a challenge here: Zen Master Seung Sahn, the Dalai Lama, Zen Master Ji Bong, Zen Master Jeong Ji, Gil Fronsdal, Sharon Salzberg, Howie Cohn, Marie Mannschatz, Sojun Roshi, Amma, Joel Osteen, and Braco whose profound kindness and sincerity, along with that of my friends', encouraged me on the spiritual path.

To people who supported me with kind ears listening to my poetry: the Sufi Camp of the South Bay community, the Vision Masters, and the Silk Road Chai Shop. After a late afternoon hike on Mount Shasta, there after dusk, I dropped in by chance to the Silk Road to find an open mic and open ears to read more than a handful of poems from the manuscript in front of a live audience for the very first time.

To a talented mutual co-conspirator Mary Gow whose challenge on Halloween created an unexpected ripple, ripening this faster than expected.

To all of you and lastly to our fledgling meditation community: What would I have done without all of you, your love, encouragement and blessings?

In honor of poets, musicians and one of the greatest poets to ever grace our earth, who other than Rumi, Jalaluddin Rumi, the Sufi mystic from the 13th century: His profound work is so alive, speaking to us intimately eight centuries later.

To Gandhi, Mandela, King, Rosa Parks: You who still point to the way to love. We need your wisdom now more than ever.

Lastly to all of us: Change and love are possible because of us, because of truth, because we believe. It is my great wish that this book may help call us back to our own hearts.

May this be a spark to keep any one of many flames burning brightly anywhere in the world. Lofty? Maybe. Why aim for anything less for all of us?

Wishing you bright illumination and blessings on your journey.

Muskie

8 December 2016
San Francisco

PS. Every word tense, every missing punctuation, it's not a mistake, it's all on purpose... like the misuse of like.

Books or films by teachers and friends mentioned in Acknowledgments:

Cohn, Howard. *Invitation to Meditation: How to Find Peace Wherever You Are*. San Francisco: Chronicle, 2016.

Feng, Anita. *Sid*. Somerville, MA: Wisdom, 2015.

Fronsdal, Gil. *The Dhammapada: A New Translation of the Buddhist Classic with Annotations*. Boston: Shambhala, 2005.

Joy of Life. Braco. 2016.

Lama, Dalai, and Desmond Tutu. *The Book of Joy: Lasting Happiness in a Changing World*. New York: Avery, an Imprint of Penguin Random House, 2016.

Mannschatz, Marie. *Lieben Und Loslassen: Durch Meditation Das Herz öffnen*. Berlin: Theseus-Verl., 2002.

Old Plum Mountain - The Berkeley Zen Center, Life Inside the Gate. Dir. Edwin Herzog. Perf. Sojun Roshi, Shunryu Suzuki Roshi. 2012.

Osteen, Joel. *I Declare: 31 Promises to Speak over Your Life*. New York, NY: FaithWords, 2012.

Rosenbaum, Robert. *Walking the Way: 81 Zen Encounters with the Tao Te Ching*. Boston: Wisdom Publications, 2013.

Sahn, Zen Master Seung, and Hyon Gak, Sunim. *The Compass of Zen*. Boston: Shambhala, 1997.

Salzberg, Sharon. *Lovingkindness: The Revolutionary Art of Happiness*. Boston: Shambhala, 1995.

Walton, Todd, and Mindy Toomay. *The Writer's Path: A Guidebook for Your Creative Journey: Exercises, Essays, and Examples*. Berkeley: Ten Speed, 2000.

PREFACE

Reading slowly
within the stillness
within your own being
Reveling in being
Letting the words be

Breathing in the spaces
between

Without figuring it out,
without thinking
yet still breathing.

Just like this is Buddha...

Now how's
your breathing?

If the mind's been
shaken or is distracted
however,
gently wait,
walking will rest
heart & mind.

Slow, slow
five breaths here आर्ष toward freedom
Even reading in the wonder and
silence of nature
Bringing soothing to your being.
Unifying being.
Absorbing slowly
each line
drinking in your own being...
sinking into nature.
Slowing into sipping a
half-caf Americano or green tea.

May we return to present time,
to our inner beings being.

MUSKIE FIELDS

आर्ष

You wonder
Fact or fiction?

It's all much stranger than that.

आर्ष

Our earth
kissed us into life.
Now you with
your presence.

आर्ष

Thanks for
moistening
my heart
until it
glistens

with a thousand
humble tears
of gratitude

आर्ष

Love -- It's the only thing that matters...

Attention costs nothing
yet, it's the most desirable---
it's what love is really made from.

आर्ष

Love, the nectar of
Gods[1] and Them
visited like a
Heavenly arrow to
heart & soul.

All I could do is let it be,
Struggle and then let it be.

[1] Gods, Goddesses, God, the universal source,
oneness, the Akashic record, whatever you call it.

आर्ष

That day
Annie Lamott
Spiritually
Sprinkled us with
love, joy, encouragement,
happiness and just being herself.

Word by word[1].

[1] Lamott, Anne. *Bird by Bird: Some Instructions on Writing and Life*. Sydney, Australia: Scribe Publications, 2008.

आरुष

Already taking a year off
A year to the day
A car collided totaling mine
Preventing me from
leaving this tiny hamlet.

Rolling down the window
Your warm brown eyes
peering in, meeting mine
Life again, it's
Stranger than Fiction[1].

---

[1] *Stranger Than Fiction*. Dir. Marc Forster. 2006.

आर्ष

When his eyes caught mine
He a mere three or
four years on earth,
skin tan and dark
Just a child some might say.

With deep eyes of innocent kindness
He peered right through me:
A clearing so profound
opening my being.
Turning away, full with tears.

Leaving me vulnerable to love.

आर्ष

In silence...

A short distance away
Fedora'd, he hiked with me,
Up the mountain source,
On the spirit mountain
While this consciousness
Bubbled an ineffable
Stream.

आर्ष

When it was time
for the soul call,
On calling in
the Beloved...

In the midst of that work
you said, "Call me."

आर्ष

Romancing the words
Music to the heart
Blue notes fluting aloft
like a garden scent.
Knowing of this love
draped under
a turquoise shawl
peering in...
You called out "Krishna!"
And so this story began.

आर्ष

Just one look from you
and waves, pulses of sobs
throb through me
washing away mistakes.

Just one look from you
and my whole world is
set right.

Nose stinging with
gratitude for such a
glance.

आरुष

When I lose my heart
When I make a mistake
I feel I've lost you--
who are my heart.

Please let me be
kind always.
That you, my friend,
may wish to take me
with you.
Always.

आर्ष

There's no logic to it
in the conventional
sense

It's not like I set out
with such an intention.
But this is just so.

I can't seem to change it
without harming myself.

A move away--- is like
hurting my own heart.

The more connected
I am with it.
The more everything
is set right.

आर्ष

Our hearts beating
a love poem.
Songs to the celestial beings
a fountain of blessings.
A bridge, a portal to
the hem of healing,
of beneficent love.

We are all drenched in the divine.

आर्ष

Take me with you---
You say you've heard that before.

I love you with all my heart I say--
Has anyone said that before?

But alas,
silent
I haven't uttered a word.

आर्ष

Please don't let me forget this love
Breathing my heart.
Without it, the spring is barren.

With it,
fountains of creativity
long past midnight.

आर्ष

Like reuniting with this love
In this temple
I wept

आर्ष

That night in the downpour, like a magi
You wore the coat of my father
heading away from the temple
drenched in the rain in black garments
I longed to follow you.

आर्ष

May we sleep tonight.
You in my dreams
are reading there next to me.
The lamp flickers.

I cannot wait to hear you
Tell me a story.
Then may I
Sleep in your arms tonight.

आर्ष

Just that love exists--
A miracle.
Sky reaching high.
The hummingbird dives
Full speed
Expertly diverting disaster
In a high pitched chirp.
A flight of great risk
He dazzles his
Love interest.

How is it possible?

आर्ष

The body knows
something:
It can't be told.

If you are here
you'd drive 50 mph
up a winding road---
over White's Hill
Like a wild moth
fevered in spring.

Even the rain
doesn't forget.

आर्ष

In his blue jean shirt
At the entryway of the divine
His look,
Stealing me with his eyes

आर्ष

My heart nearly forgot
In busy-ness
But tears in a rain storm
fell and persisted
Bringing all back to me
not to forget

आर्ष

You said be the giant dove
in the bullet proof vest.
These are your friends and
Your best friend is guess?

आर्ष

Making an offering
is my will
This triggers you.
Thinking this means
I'll die before you.
Friends exploit
this fear in you.
Afraid they are to lose you.

As if they would.

आर्ष

Nothing to be done about it.
Underneath, it does not change.
Just seeing a person vacuum is enough!

Ah, vacuuming.
It's much stranger than fiction[1].
Ah, vacuuming. To vacuuming!

[1] *Stranger Than Fiction*. Dir. Marc Forster. 2006.

आर्ष

He said things I can't
tell you here
They were the beloved
wishes dear
They did however
reach these ears.

आर्ष

A lady moving
entertains the frequent
in full view of a seated 300
She roasts alive
what fun in a drive
to end this love
Who but -guess-
would initiate?

आर्ष

Farmers intermingle in the market
Among flowers, meat, fruits and cheese.
There I am gathering snap peas
when I realize how people go about
selecting all these vegetables and fruits.

They take only the perfect,
unbruised, unbitten by bugs.
How would the rest of the
peas become their destiny?
I wondered, eyes brimming.

Barbara, farm grown herself
joins me over the bins
while I share the
Epiphany over Peas.

आ॒र्ष

Standing at the farmer's market
A man selling grapes tells a
customer:

> Chicken shit is fertilizer
> for these champagne grapes.

In a moment it dawns on me:

> We worry about shit.
> How frightened we are about
> any contact with the stuff.

> Yet manure vitalizes,
> inspiring our food to grow
> It is our very nourishment
> then, feeding us:

This is the irony about shit.
How surprising it is:
This "shit" leads to our growth,
Aliveness and even...
To our Awakening.

आर्ष

I love this tree--- it's just being itself.

आरष

Put your awakened mind to work.
Imagine the love missing to a child –
The difference can be whether they
end up in prison or in the presidency[1].

[1] My Brother's Keeper, an initiative of President
Obama, will continue post presidency, while the
President returns to having a blast, getting more
sleep and being only human.

आर्ष

Dreaming of you in a
Fairfax café
You suddenly appear.
I'm stunned.
You sit down.
Anxiously,
We stumble speaking
in a somewhat halting
conversation.

Better try breathing first
next time
Be utterly speechless
just gaze.

आर्ष

Maybe you've failed at everything:
Human relations, work,
driving, taxes, finances...
Having a sense of humor at times with
challenging people, housing arrangements.
Even entry into the most precious
Church, Temple, Mosque or Dharma Hall.

And so my dear heart,
sit then and heed this:

>All these seeming failures
>may be the making of a
>great catastrophe of
>love without measure---
>Who knows.
>Perhaps
>for the whole world and
>for all time[1].

Even you can't stop it.

---

[1] We are connected to the whole world in unseen
ways and some times we cannot begin to
comprehend our ability to have an effect on it.

आर्ष

Failure, perhaps
undeniably the greatest teacher.
Hear my confession to you in the world:
Failing even at a love
without my choosing,
without my intention or knowing.
Beyond all knowing.

Yet still, I've failed even this.

आर्ष

[1] A "dictionary attack" is a method of cracking passwords relying on repetitive attempts by trying every word in a dictionary.

As if I could make life happen...
I tried this method
toward living ---
The dictionary attack[1].

And then I realized... I forgot
about the universe, about grace,
about surrender, about prayer.

Unable to hear the whispers
telling me where to go
I wasted precious moments
to remember this lesson

आर्ष

All my trying and
Striving
Failed.

Once I relaxed,
I found you here
With me.

आर्ष

Sublime body

Always the last to know --
Logic understands Nothing.

Beyond thinking
The body knows its truth.
There's nothing more sublime
than this--
Even the suffering here is sweet,
like late plums in Woodacre
and fresh baby grapes off the vine.

Only I miss you.
When will you visit
so I may be speechless
before you and

serve you tea?

Even a word can't say
anything. So I
bumble about
mixing words with myth
in silence.

While only my heart
knows so very little about
this territory
Still, I go on.

आर्ष

The Bridge[1] to the Heart

It doesn't go away.
In time
and space--
I only forget a little.

Still, on my mind
day in, day out.
Evening, sunrise,
evening. Repeat.

I can't forget.
If someone asks me out,
my heart cries out its protest.
Sober, I realize I can try it.

But, still, in my heart
It's only this.

[1] Penned on the way to cross a San Francisco
Bay Area Bridge.

आर्ष

You are like a gift
Still *unwrapped*
Which I look forward to

Even when you are stubborn
Even then, I love you still.

आर्ष

Honey--
Please stop your wandering
around and come home.

Where is Moses
when you need him?

You must tell the truth.

आर्ष

One night the coyotes
howling the hunt
high on
ridges of Woodacre

Nearby deer
spotted a thicket.
In one mind,
I too wanted to leap
into the thicket.

Then I realized
all at once
The obvious:
I was not a deer.

आर्ष

An arsenal of attempts on my heart
I longed for you
Yet, surrounded by a
moat of social commitments,
you would not surrender your heart.

There you allowed me to suffer this way.

आर्ष

i moved on
but my heart --
it just
stayed

twinkling...
in the ancient
beauty
in the awe
and wonder
of it all

आर्ष

Finally life ran aground here.

I left the hamlet, leaving the
tribe of deer behind.

Among the deer too
the community of
skunks, jackrabbits
and coyotes.

Among them, I found home.

आर्ष

Leaving town
on that moving day

The writing
cited literally
on the wall
Clear as day

There--
Mounted on the *rear* of this truck
facing the 580 traffic
following behind.
There-- this prodigious sign
proclaims itself in giant letters:

> *A way would open*
> *where there was no way.*

So certain was this truck with
its traveling inspiration.

आर्ष

Across the bay,
Upon arriving on Grizzly Peak

Ennobled in regalia
Majestically
the full grown buck greeted me
twice that very night.

Apparently
He'd received notice
from the tiny hamlet of deer,
Now I was among them
on this high peak.

So like a shaman in
his neck of the woods,
he stood welcoming me there
twice on this dark
September starlit night.

आर्ष

The Moon reminded me
How much I love
Thee:

Sand delivered from Stars,
Earth swept up in the Universe,
Starlight from the Heavens.
Water from crystal ice.
Imbued with blessings.

Incomprehensible.

आर्ष

Your ride out front
You found me bantering
inside Culture Shock[1].

Outside you asked me
what I thought of
the woman teacher *married* to
her teacher.

Not getting your meaning
I only said it sounded like
Good Morning America.

This perhaps you took as a no.

[1] An interesting shop originally in Fairfax, CA.

आर्ष

Make a commitment, he said.

Start telling the truth, I said.

आर्ष

Uncountable times he is on
my trail tracking my scent.

Always one step ahead
he knows where
I go next.

He hints in his way
nosing me in the direction
of my heart.

आर्ष

I could not find the place
Where I belonged.
Elsewhere, I looked everywhere.

Nothing made sense.
Because the place I belonged,
it seemed, was in your heart.

आर्ष

My heart slung down low
Beneath dreams of Love
Never Arrived.

Still I could feel my heart
This love.

Nothing else seemed to do.

आर्ष

Nothing Happened?
Then, sure.
Nothing Happened.

If it is Nothing
I only wish this Nothing would
happen, everywhere, for all beings.

आर्ष

They want me to disembody
the Beloved in my mind.

"This would help how?" you ask.

His blood, guts, bones, lymph,
snot and bile would help me
realize the impermanence of
love, of the beloved, of me.
And devote myself to practice I would.

Instead.
Was I amazed about
the magic, astounding miracles,

the wonder and impossibility of he.

How could a vat of blood, pile of
guts, white sticks & cage of bones,
sinews, gooey snots, viscous lymph
be this?

How much more appreciation
sprung forth for the mystery
of being, of existence and
even more of love, and the beloved.

Thus, these instructions failed me.

आर्ष

You said feelings are important
You said to trust you
Then you left,
nowhere to be found.

Upset.
You tricked me again
it seemed.
Then I realized it:

At last
once again my heart
gazes back at me.

आर्ष

When I stopped running
The world became still.
A deeper well,
Here was happiness.

Finally I could hear
What was lost in the
Music, in the Busy-ness.

Calling me back to my
Heart.

आर्ष

At times, you acted
so strangely.
Never occurred to me
until later what this was:

How crazy love makes us.
And the wish for *Bodhicitta*[1].

[1] The great wish to save sentient beings from suffering, helping them to practice and progress on the path of awakening. In the US, Bodhicitta is pronounced boe dee cheetah or boe dee chittah.

आर्ष

Even in this state -- mad at you--
there's the buzz of electric
current as you walk by me.
The spark across a synapse.

Leaping between
heart to heart.

आर्ष

When you stop what hinders you
You won't believe the energy you'll have.
You won't believe how much
the whole world is waiting to welcome
You back to life.

Turn off the TV.
Turn down the worry & fear.
Untangle yourself from the web.

Discover the magic all around you.
It's in every moment.
You'll never believe what's
available for you to see.
You'll never regret it.

आर्ष

If you love this breath
You'll know the truth.

आरुष

Find out about love
About wonder and delight.

The Kingdom of Heaven
Is truly within
Believe it
Be it.
This is the only now
We have.

There is no past now
or future now.
Only here. This.

आर्ष

Not finding my home
Yet still there is this love.

Better to be free than
Be without this.

आर्ष

If you love something
You are that[1].
How could it be otherwise?
Even the mirror neurons
Tell the truth.

[1] You are that love.

आर्ष

There's no time to wait
Like more water for your body
This love is like the delight you
Will one day take in breathing
When you finally meet your
Heart:

    You will kiss the ground
    You walk on.

Your eyes will blur in moisture
Regarding the 10,000 mysteries,
The flutter of birds,
Scare of the skunk,
Scent of pine needles,
Soft eyes of deer

The majesty

of the human body—with every bone
connected to other bones—
The blunders and pleasures of our
speech and actions.

From this vantage: A miracle.

आर्ष

The more present
you become
the light changes
as if swirls of energy
to this presence.

Magical, you are the center of it.

आर्ष

Luminescent green hills
lit with golden sunlight
This glow calls me.

Do we surrender or
do we push fate?

आर्ष

Their thoughts or –
my thoughts of their thoughts
drove me away from you.

Like that night in the ballroom
Why did you forsake me?

आर्ष

The Golden Bridge[1]
Symbol and inspiration of the entire world
One *massive* set of candles
Lit end to end to celebrate the
Wedding of San Francisco to Marin.
Flowing like Niagara Falls
A great expanse of beauty and delight
Like the heart opening for the
world to share

Such *magnificence.*

Nearly unbearable to see this without you.
Twinges of pain, poignant tonight.

[1] *Golden Bridge.* Braco. 2016.

आर्ष

"Where have you been?"
Laurie Jan exclaimed with
a deep inflection.

Like something
supernatural was afoot.

आर्ष

Hidden from anyone's view.

It's evening past twilight,
There are people winding up conversations
Yet, only I see you drive at high speeds
in giant circles in the temple parking lot.

Like a "teenage broncin' buck"[1]
You circle round
Exhilarating and hilarious ---
Astounding!

How is it that I'm the only one
who ever sees you?

[1] Don McLean. "American pie." *American Pie.* 1971.

आर्ष

This is the third time.
Once at a gala
There at a parade
Here on a spirited trail.
Sweeping yourself below me in a.

You scare me that
you tease me
once again with
wanting you.

आर्ष

Thanks for
letting me
love you --
even if it was
like a
bubble,
insubstantial:
Like a dream --
not to be taken
for reality.

But still
my heart
glistens
from the love
you allowed
me
to entertain.

For you,

it goes on.

For me,
I sit in
wonder
at the
majesty
of it all.

Insubstantial &
like a dream,
I go on:
Treasuring
this
bubble:
insubstantial
& like a
dream.

आर्ष

Find your house
You challenged.
Like those skilled in finding
guidance through the high seas
by dint of their cojones.

Parking suddenly
not knowing where you lived
walking directly to your house.

Marveling, stunned.
Your car parked in the drive,
clearly displaying your plate.
Standing there shocked in silence:
This is where you live.

How much I wanted to...
How I could have knocked...
Then I worried

would you be
shocked or accept me?
I could go no further.
Turning about face
realizing some many
more steps needed
before we could
both feel safe

Fearless

आर्ष

A thousand secret transmissions
And only one nearby seer sage
knows about them
Besides me?

You race in circles like a teenager
under people's noses and they
Still don't see you?

But you won't admit anything ---
Even your closest friends
Don't know.

आर्ष

You stole my heart,
A masked Bandit. Like a raccoon
With dinner from the grill,
You dined on my love for you.

आर्ष

How to trust?

It's baffling what to do next.
All we can do is let go and
find those who are
willing to return our love
right in the great wide open[1]

[1] *Great Wide Open*. Dir. Jared Leto. 2016.

MUSKIE FIELDS

आर्ष

My heart broken.
Afraid.
You left without a
hug or a kiss.

My heart sank with
yours... deep inside
your coat.

There is this sadness
while you leave.

I love you so and still
you don't know...
This hidden truth.

आर्ष

Here I am
present
and lost.

Just breathing
simply breathing.
Still I will go somewhere
tonight without you.

I will enjoy my friends
all of life hanging in a
balance: as if some
part of the universe is

slightly amiss.

Little by little, I will find
a way forward
inches at a time.

Not knowing
where I belong,
if your love will
ever return or
if you ever loved me.

आर्ष

When I realized he's not coming back
Tears fell like rain.
What a fool I've been.

Which fool is it? you ask

आर्ष

When she finds the ones
she's loved and cared for
Not able to respond to her heart
Unsharing as friends
She goes looking for her true friends.

आर्ष

Trying so hard
to no avail.

Thank you universe
for sending love
here.

Send one who could
but doesn't want to
live without me.

आर्ष

Unable to find my place, my home
I went house-surfing.
A true adventure of spirit,
These were the knees
I was looking for[1].

[1] To bow to the earth, to life, to the beauty
and delight of awareness and consciousness,
to love.

आर्ष

When there is no grasping

to what arises in the mind
and no belief in it

One is free in great bliss[1]

<hr />

[1] This doesn't mean that things don't exist.
We'll still wantwisdom for wise actions.

MUSKIE FIELDS

आर्ष

Belonging here,
but where I'll go?
I am moving to nowhere
for the time being.

There, I'll stay in wonder.

आर्ष

Hearing the rustling of leaves
in an underbrush near a
Franklin Street sidewalk:

Even a rat
needs a place
she can rest her head and call home.

आर्ष

Rafiki you call me friend.
I call this safe haven,
home until I go home.

आर्ष

Ask me, do I know what I am doing
I've got no idea
Let's give earth a chance[1]
Let's give love a chance
However like a baby deer on
Spindly legs at the start.

[1] Tag line from the first Earth Day celebration in DC, Spring 1970.

आर्ष

Warm sultry evening past twilight
bathes sweet meadow grasses.
Trees and earth accept
Bountiful summer rain here.
Crickets, in waves, sing at fever pitch.

An open window:
Female moans and sighs waft
by neighbors and passersby.
Some listen embarrassed, some intrigued.

आर्ष

I've found a joy
in landing nowhere
And yet still

It'd be great to come home.

आर्ष

All of this is gone now.
like a mist
Disappeared.
Still, the love within me
stays.
Awakened by
love.

आर्ष

It's long ago now
It doesn't matter any more
Yet it was the time of my life.
At the time.

आर्ष

Where is my Julia Child
in all of this?
She's cooking up a storm of love
and tasty dreams
Apron'd in the kitchen.

आर्ष

You drive me crazy[1]
pushing every button.
The last button more
deadly than the rest.

And still. Against all odds
My heart springs forth
unflappable energy for you.

Nuts, huh?

[1] A metaphor for being triggered. While the stimulus
is outside, the trigger is in us. When we are triggered,
we still are still responsible for how we respond.
That said, if it seems sensible to do so, we also may
let someone know how we feel about something
which triggers us.

आर्ष

You left me wondering
whether you love me.
I worry day and night
about this.

Insecure, forlorn, fearing loss.
When will it end?

As soon as I call all the Buddhas
and Bodhisattvas[1]...

In comes, Annie Lamott.
"Help, Thanks, Wow."[2]

"Pray to be humble enough
to ask for help," she says.

[1] Bodhisattvas: literally beings who hear the cries
of the world and act to save them from suffering
(US pronunciation boe dee sahtt vahs)
[2] Lamott, Anne. *Help, Thanks, Wow: The Three
EssentialPrayers*. New York: Riverhead, 2012.

आर्ष

Duking it out with
Paper tigers
Some real
Some of my own making

All just paper.

आर्ष

Every zig
a corresponding zag.
No telling where this is headed.
Certainly, this is the Longest Way Home[1].

[1] McCarthy, Andrew. *The Longest Way Home:
One Man's Quest for the Courage to Settle Down.*
New York: Free Press, 2012.

आर्ष

"It's not easy being a mystic,"
Halim said to me recently.
His remark landed like
compassion soothing the soul.

Ah... is that what this is?
I am, he is, she is, we are mystics.
That explains a lot.

आर्ष

How will I meet the beloved
everywhere, anywhere?

When will he be willing to
see me, to meet me?

Still,
moved with compassion,
Now I see you fully.

Please tell me your truth.

आर्ष

You don't answer and you
don't say no either.

Am I teetering on disaster?

Or is this your way of being
sure if I have the courage of
my convictions?

What is this with
one who hides his truth?

I feel scared.

आर्ष

Frightened?

Please don't fear me.
I also fear you.
Like Pi[1], there's a tiger
in the boat with me.

Will you eat me alive,
spare me or throw me
overboard?

Can we tame some wild and
keep some wild wild?

Wow, what great risk
involved really.

[1] *Life of Pi*. Dir. Ang Lee. 2012.

आर्ष

Heart on the line.
Will you spare me
or take my life?

Do I fit somewhere
in your truth?
Will you have mercy
on me and my uncountable
mistakes?

आरुष

In my being,
it's like you are my home.

Tried to forget you.
And every time I got close,
your memory kept me from it.

It's like somewhere
deep in my heart,
my heart is made of fibers
from your heart.

What to do?

While I am happily everywhere,
there's no place like
in your arms or in your heart.

But I suspect
you've known that all along.

आर्ष

Nothing's more interesting than
the whispers of the soul.
Finally I know what I want.

Where are you?
Sometimes we need to be
really far from it before
we realize what's important to us.

आर्ष

Leaving no discernible trace
for the ordinary to see
only the sages knew the truth.

Yet everywhere
there are tracks in my heart.
A thousand gossamer threads
bond me to him

Under the glow of the lamplight
his sleeves rolled up
passionate, he wove dreams---
a magic creation.

Bless his heart, for without him,
I would not know love.

आर्ष

From before the ball
well to now
in the latter perhaps
there is a reason.

In this tribe is it that
loving's okay for them,
for others, it is treason?

आर्ष

All of us know but we don't say
You know, but you can't say
I know, but I won't say.

All know and we don't say.
A code of honor?

When will the place which speaks of
Truth, say the truth?

आर्ष

Finally, when torment
rose to overwhelming,
When I ask you
Why you are reading my mind
You say,
"Because of what you said to Amma."

आर्ष

But you weren't even *there*
That evening

When suddenly in a flash, like a reflex,
some part of my soul said,
"I love ____ " and your name
spontaneously sprung up.

Just then, Amma's
eyes darted at mine.

The irony?
What or who was on my mind?
        Seth, a Medical Qigong Master.

आर्ष

The Lama, Amma, the Essence man
The Heart as Wide as the World, Lumière
The Bhikkhu with a Bodhi mind & the
Green light enlightening the Gulch

Mystifying...
without speaking
How do these seers know this--
what is this-- between us?
Their kindly knowing like a blessing,
soothes my heart

Some don't know me but they know.
Is the heart's transmission
unstoppable, as if
imprinted on the wind?

One day we will measure
this subtle energy:
our own living gravitational fields.

आर्ष

Did my best and
still I couldn't
outrun myself

I can no more
lose this love
than remove
my own heart

आर्ष

A second mistake
In this lifetime?
Being away from
The truth and who
Your deepest
Soul loves?

Will you cheat and deceive
Yourself again
This lifetime?

आर्ष

You asked me to trust you,
But this way and that
swerving
you confuse all of us
trying to follow the plot.

In the end, I am sure
we are all amazed
at your genius.

आर्ष

We know the truth.

That truth
calls us
in the night.

आर्ष

Sound asleep
In the wee hours of night

The sound of my name
Presents from outside

  As clear as day.
  But it is night.

A few nights later the light overhead
starts working after months--
Years even, I'm told.
Turning itself on,
Enlightening the
whole room during sleep.

What's going on here?

आर्ष

Just allow yourself
some being
time.

What?
you say
Stop doing?

Yes, let the universe
Be for a while.

आर्ष

Sacred heart
covenant with the universe,
the infinite divine...
I won't give up
on love.

आर्ष

Each time I try to go another way
or find one...

There you are already noticing
Already one step ahead of me

Seems you own a Marauder's Map[1]
to know so much of where I'll be.
Like the one bequeathed to
Harry Potter by Fred and George Weasley.

[1] Rowling, J. K., GrandPré, Mary. *Harry Potter and the Prisoner of Azkaban*. New York: Arthur A. Levine, 1999.

　　　MUSKIE FIELDS

आर्ष

At some point
you're stuck with
no other alternative
But to accept yourself.

आर्ष

You and I
we climbed together
to the source of love.

For this,
I am forever
grateful.

आर्ष

"He is influenced by his friends," I said.
"Why does he let himself be
influenced by them?" asked
my new Berber heart-friend.

After a moment in silence,
the Berber wise man said:

> *"I wouldn't allow my friends to*
> *influence me. I would listen*
> *to them and decide for myself."*

At this simple answer, I wept.

आर्ष

The Berber wise man said to his friend:

> *"If you see her*
> *she's my friend,*
> *take care of her."*

So cared for was I by this one who hardly
knew me except in an energetic intuitive
spirit of friendship of the heart.

Remembering this later,
I was moved for the kindly
love that was so natural.
Such a kind heart
from such a far away land.

आर्ष

When I told my sister of this
She said in her way
including a scripture verse:
the universe was
making things
right.

आर्ष

When I started acting
a *little* crazy---
suddenly
it dawned on me
why you had been acting crazy.

I thought you were
acting kind of strange some of that time.

Now I knew this crazy feeling---
A new visitor to me.
Ah, so that was it.
You appeared to be possessed by
this crazy feeling too.

Powerlessness over the beloved--
That can make you crazy.

आर्ष

You arrive two nights that week
awake within sleeping dreams.

You, bringing
two magnums of Champagne
Your head falling into my lap
While I endeavor to read and
remember the note in French
It read:

      "Mis en Feu"[1]

On another evening you spun
me around dancing.

Each time I started a word
to mention this, you stopped
me before I could utter anything.

[1] Translation from the French: "set on fire"
  or "put on fire".

आर्ष

Peeved at you for
What is in dreams

These visits barely
a substitute
for the real,
I was miffed at you.

Fun or unusual as it is--
There's no exchanging
them for the existential real.

आर्ष

You think you can shut
out destiny?
Or that Shamans
can help?

Even Shaman prayers
can't change
destiny:

They simply open the way for destiny.

आर्ष

My friend Bing told me this story.

She had everything, the house,
the car, even the sex was excellent.
She dangled more things in front of him.
My friend's family wanted him,
even begged him to marry this woman.

For seven years he tried.
In the end, he couldn't do it.

It was his soul.

He was missing something ineffable.
Something deeper, indescribable.
It wasn't logical.
But at the soul level he knew.
He knew he would be missing
something his whole life.
So, he couldn't do it.

आर्ष

Happy &
living at this mystifying address.

The address I belong to is in
the true beloved's arms.

"Who else do you marry
but the one who pulls you
off the stage?"[1, 2]

'Kiteshvara[3]
"They say you
marry the one
you can't live without."[4]

[1] Miller, Donald. *Scary Close: Dropping the Act and Finding True Intimacy.* Nashville, TN: Nelson, 2014, p. 3.
[2] This is the one who encourages and won't even settle for anything less than you're being your true self.
[3] Short for the Sanskrit name Avalokiteshvara, the Bodhisattva who literally percieves sound and hears the cries of the world. Aka. Chenrezig in Tibetan, Guan Shi Yin in Chinese, Kwan Seum Bosal in Korean, Quan Âm in Vietnamese, Kanzeon in Japanese.
[4] *Maneater.* Dir. Peter Werner. 2005.

आर्ष

How mystical we are.

Do we have the patience
to teach each other our
languages?

आर्ष

When Jim Nabors[1]
honors his love,
finally open to the air,
A mere[2] 35 years in the making
I feel this pang of being
touched by how long
it is to keep such a secret.

And then... why can't
my love be right out loud--
right here in the great wide open[3]?

[1] Jim Nabors, actor, most renowned for his role
from 1962-1969 in *The Andy Griffith Show* and
in *Gomer Pyle, USMC*, as Gomer Pyle.
[2] Mere is not at all mere here.
[3] *Great Wide Open*. Dir. Jared Leto. 2016.

आर्षं

She said to me, "You're dripping with
good deeds." Then she admitted
she wasn't fond of the word
dripping, but it did not matter.
Hearing her kind words, I was
dripping with tears from her love.

"Who was it?" you ask.
Why it was my own sister,
a mystic, a Christian,
a true practitioner of the faith.

Imagine a love like that
between sisters.

आर्ष

When we talked further about
this, she clarified, your hands are
filled with good deeds.

How do you know? I asked
since she lives in a beach town
in New England.

I can see them, she said.

आर्ष

Every single person,
even all the great
sages will die.

Like kindness,
A bright light
defended me.

Said you sent no cards or letters
What could you expect?

आर्ष

Another brave and earnest.
Innocent.
He said, Wow,
why not this one?

You walked out on
his kind appreciative rant.

आर्ष

Long before this
Uncountable times
you waited at the deli
hoping I'd stop by
on the drive by this tiny hamlet.

Remembering this---
All your trying
I lament missing you.

आर्ष

Time with someone else
only shows me how much
I love you.

If it is you,
be with me
heart body and soul.

आर्ष

How to have faith in the
unseen and not let a
fog of doubts overcome
a luminous mind.

आर्षं

Plant unwatered
untended
How can I bring it back
to life?

Missing this heart.

आर्ष

Please don't go everywhere
until you remember
your true face.

Your home is here with me.

आर्षं

My heart just about
lost itself one day.

Was I dying? I felt incredibly
physically strange.

Or was I just on the wrong track
going away from destiny?

Jean the Iphone programmer--
the least likely to explain it
said: "Your body knows."

आर्ष

An unexpected meeting
In a petite Peet's café
His home half the world away,
the Sufi Master from Jerusalem[1]
blesses me while moved,
I'm sobbing.

What was that?
Did he just say

> *All my wishes*
> *would come true*
> or
> May all my wishes
> come true?

[1] He was, as it turns out, the Sufi Master from Jerusalem, Sidi al Jamal, who since then yielded his spirit. May peace be upon him.

आर्ष

Every moment away from you
a loss, a death.
While I resolve my fear and
become fearless

आर्ष

People say be careful
what you wish for
As if what you wished for
was fraught with danger or
tigers, lions and bears...

May this be the danger
to enlighten us & all beings.

आर्ष

How to be fearless?
You want courage?
Inspiration? Love?
Justice?

Jackie Robinson, 42[1].

Need I say more?

---

[1] *42: The Jackie Robinson Story*. Dir. Brian Helgeland.
2013. Branch Rickey hires Jackie Robinson
making history breaking the race barrier in Major
League Baseball.

आर्ष

You a puzzle, unsolved,
need love.
If change helps you arrive
At your own truth

Then in the land of impermanence,
throw your hat over
the wall of tribal wishes for constancy:

Composting--
on the path to inner wisdom
throws us back on ourselves
unifying the inner hu[1].

How does it happen? You wonder.

Only don't know[2].
It's a mystery
then...
To me and to you.

[1] Divine Presence
[2] Master, Seung Sahn Zen. Only Don't Know:
   The Teaching Letters of Zen Master Seung Sahn.
   USA: Primary Point,

आर्ष

While with word by word
You say you need someone
to watch over you

My heart dripping in tears
A mess
You're surrounded
I can't approach

Head bowed, dipped
hiding runny nose
Departing into
the evening's
San Francisco mist.

It is there
where I left my heart.

आर्ष

Karmapa[1] in the city of
San Francisco expounding on
Great love, Great compassion.
We must try to save someone
even at great risk to ourselves.

That's *Bodhicitta*[2].

[1] His Holiness the 17th Gyalwang Karmapa, head of
the Karma Kagyu school of Tibetan Buddhism,
paraphrase, San Francisco, March 19, 2015.
[2] The great wish to save sentient beings from
suffering, helping them to attain or progress on
the path of awakening.

आर्ष

Now what is this?

Your behavior
worse than ever.
Acting out,
impossible, incorrigible.

Talking about your
speech and actions
like many wives' and
husbands'
complaining...

Telling my sister all.

The man of light looked
sad as I told him thus.
Sad even now to report it here.

आर्ष

A dream once sometime before
I so dreamed a string emerged
in this couch-like scene
while you writhed, your side on this floor.

When I asked you about it years before,
we didn't then get past this open door.

आर्ष

And wait--
There's the minister of pain.
The rules of his game
aren't about truth and honesty.
It's at once gene-rat-ing,
protecting positions and secret shame.
So caught, like an addict one can hate.
My heart once recovered, quivered with
sadness to see some so afflicted in this fate.

आर्ष

Years before a Bodhisattva[1] scribe
said it within a loving theme
someone might be trying to
hurt her...

Oh, what could he mean?

आर्ष

Are you being saved?
Or just further
down the path of
unredeemed?

You see awakening is not
a one directional arrow
as much as it
might have seemed.

[1] The Bodhisattva is a being who hears the cries
   of beings in the world and works to assist them
   in relieving their suffering.

आर्ष

Separated
from the heart
it's not an ordinary death.

They say it's living like a ghost
Taken over by an undetected darkness.

While still living life...
Undeniably, it's like a theft.

आर्ष

As kind as a kingdom is/is not
Like Cinderella[1],
Lost my faith
in faith and being kind.

Like Sleeping Beauty[2]
Poisoned, I rest asleep.

[1] *Cinderella*. Dir. Kenneth Branagh. 2015.
screenplay, Chris Weitz.
Perrault, Charles. *La Petite Pantoufle de Verre*.
1697.
[2] *Sleeping Beauty*. Dir. Clyde Geronimi. 1959.
Perrault, Charles. *La Belle Au Bois Dormant*. 1697.

आर्ष

Is this the last chance
I take to save you?
I'm wondering sadly.

As if another spirit
haunts your being
You've become
someone else unreal,
unrecognizable.

It's hard to watch this.
Am I mistaken or
is it fakery?
Do you or anyone else know it?

आर्ष

Like Saint Peter
You deny knowing me thrice.

आर्ष

Even the beloved Milarepa[1]
recognizes the harm he enacted.
Unsettled in anxiety with
his magic and hailstorms of the dark arts,
he's troubled & distracted.

His heart filled with remorse
he seeks the true way:
the mind's liberation
freedom from suffering.
Even his teacher of the dark arts
fearing fate's reprisal,
moves to aid Milarepa in
this pressing pursuit as the
great Yogi seeks the way
to make amends with the universe.

[1] Beloved yogi of the Karma Kagyu Lineage (b. 1052).

_____ p. 152:_____

[1] In telling the truth, we still need wisdom. It's
not about sharing all without some wise
discrimination and it's not about mistruthing
to help someone get away with their actions.

आर्ष

There was and is, always a way out.
Five precepts. Ten commandments.
All rely on one fundamental principle.

All of these 5 or 10 principles have a path, a
way out, the path to liberation, to freedom.
In this post-truth world, it's a radically simple
notion. R/evolutionary really:

Telling the truth[1].

Even some murderers in life sentences
immersed, researching their inner beings.
Upon deeply knowing their flawed actions,
even these beings, may be liberated within.
When this happens they often become like
determined Bodhisattvas with the urgent and
pressing need to help all beings.

Remarkably, the only beings who cannot be
liberated are the ones who cannot tell the truth.
Thus, truth telling is unequal. Paramount.
Mission critical, even, to ultimate happiness
on the path to wisdom and freedom.

आर्ष

It came in deep,
profoundly
Clear as day.

If we hurt another, we hurt
ourselves.[1]

How could it be otherwise?

[1] The intent of an action has important implications
on the actor, whether an act is coming from ill-will
or acting to benefit the recipient(s).

आर्ष

All these US
wars proved it,
unequivocally.

QED[1]:

When we harm
Another, we harm
Ourselves[2].

Pondering here
Taking a moment...

Think about it
right here, right now.
Take the time to
Prove it to yourself.

How could it be
otherwise?

How can we absorb,
fully absorb, this truth?
To once and for all
decisively remember ---
to live this throughout
from the inside out?

आर्ष

We take our thoughts
For reality &
Then have a war with them
In our minds.

आर्ष

Love Can't Wait.
"That's one small step for man;
one giant leap for mankind."[1]
Take a stand and end the war.

Which war you say?
Iraq, Afghanistan, Egypt,
Libya, Syria, Iran?[2]
It's not the one you see out there:
It's the one you can't see in your own heart.

How do I do that you ask?
Love this breath, your heart,
find your true being.

Send love to yourself, to your neighbor &
when finally strengthened, you can, to the
very one who you believe irks you:
for the way you handle most of this-- is within.
This is "One giant leap"[1] for
human kind-ness.

[1] Neil Armstrong. July 20, 1969. Lunar landing quote.
  In memory and honor of Gene Cernan, the last man
  to walk on the moon, now touching the face of God.
[2] Yes, do care about these too, acting with wisdom.

आर्ष

In the spirit of the
Whole World is a Single Flower[1]:

When we hold ourselves
against or for, we separate.

There's a way to take a stand
without creating this division.
Not for the faint of heart[2]---
this involves holding our spirit open—
even toward what we find aversive.

That is Gandhi's Satyagra[3].
That is King's love.
It's Buddha's enlightenment.
It's Rosa Parks refusal to move on the bus.
This is Mandela, the Dalai Lama,
Aung San Suu Kyi.

This ---is courage.

[1] Zen Master Man Gong's profound expression,
  Chogye Order of South Korea.
[2] Not every situation is ours to mend.
[3] An insistence on truth with nonviolent resistance,
  to bring about social and political reforms.

आर्ष

Please don't be any more people---

Just be yourself,
Love.

आर्ष

Only go straight
don't know[1]

Instead
this path is
zig zag Zen[2, 3]

[1] Zen Master Seung Sahn. A main teaching phrase,
   1972-2004.
[2] Not to be confused with the rolling papers, Zig Zag.
[3] Badiner, Allan Hunt., and Alex Grey. *Zig Zag Zen:
   Buddhism on Psychedelics*. San Francisco: Chronicle,
   2002.

आर्ष

Is this how it happened? You ask.

Happy among loving friends
Down with love[1]
a love which doesn't meet me.
Everywhere I go, the world
freed of grasping[2] meets me.
The beloved inside meets me.

One day, the beloved finds me.

[1] *Down with Love.* Dir. Peyton Reed. 2003.
[2] When we are met with beings who are freed of grasping in the moment, and we too are in that moment freed of grasping, freed of hurrying: here is freedom, spaciousness in meeting. It would simply not be true to say this happens everywhere, but we might go through times when it seems like it as our practice develops. The fictitious I in the story can on occasion also make a mess, even if well-intended or well-meaning, or may choose strategies that fly in the face of wisdom in afterthought. But maybe these situations, too, in time, gently right themselves.

आर्ष

A while back I so dreamed
a witch she held my baby
standing in a meadow green.
No, no mind to fight her then
Not knowing how, not knowing when.
Instead King Solomon's test
would decide for both the mother of
this holy being in a rest.

आर्ष

An existential threat
is worth some crying
but losing who you love--
without again trying?

That's somehow *worse* than dying

[1] Soto: A lineage of Japanese Zen which
   stems from China.
[2] Avalokiteshvara in Tibetan (reference p. 127).

आर्ष

When all faith ebbed out of sight,
At times inspiration sprung.
A Green light in the Gulch
seeming knowing my plight
with nary a greeting,
without even meeting.
This seeing-knowing
Redeeming with kindness
Sparking faith anew.

आर्ष

Sojun expounding
on the priceless jewel

The wisdom that
cannot be taught

An unconditional friend
A peace abiding
Soto[1] Chenrezig[2]

आर्ष

Whether it was
pride or prejudice[1]
Emphatic, inflected
"It's over," she elected,
trumpeting her projected.

आर्ष

A revelation finds me.

What scares me
most?

The more my heart opens, it's
interactions lacking kindness.

[1] Austen, Jane. *Pride and Prejudice*, London:
Printed for T. Egerton, 1813.

आर्ष

Easy to have compassion for
the deeply suffering or humble,
for people without a practice.

But by what virtue to manifest
compassion for those teaching
the way out and release of suffering?
Who themselves at times seem scarcely
aware[1] when creating suffering?

[1] At times, some of us just don't see what's created.
    What the intentions are behind our actions is most
    important.

आर्ष

When I inquired about this
It was a chimney sweep
Fine man of coal
Who inspired me whilst
Speaking of compassion.

Sprouting again,
Heart bud begins blooming
Opening in a hue.

आर्ष

Later some of this lesson
came on it's own.

We've all failed at compassion at one
time or more-- maybe more-- not seeing
or knowing what to do or even perhaps
believing our thinking, that we do.

Just to even know
the wise or skillful action--
it's what this life challenges us to--
just about every moment, every day.

And with some, try and pray,
there is just simply no answer.
Nothing seems like it will ever
work, sadly and sometimes luckily,
maybe it's not our's to do.

Dancing our dance is
what we've come here to do.

आर्ष

Now a heavenly messenger
Incognito, the illustrious
Master, Don Reed,
in a chance Peet's encounter
Exhorting me not to
relinquish whatever gifts--
spirit spun hieroglyphs.

Sobbing in grief
while he oracled truth.
He knew and I knew
he was there for a reason.

आर्ष

Aiming low,
not competing
Never lose by
not even trying.
Your gifts wither, dying.

An incalculable loss.

आर्ष

Not even trying
Your gifts
Lost to the world with
Your last breath.

Megawatt power
Waylaid.
You want nothing

Yet
---Bodhicitta[1]---
The wish to save,
to benefit beings
Is something.
It's something:
A blessing
for all the world.

[1] The great wish to save sentient beings from
suffering, helping them to attain or progress
on the path of awakening.

आर्ष

You said back then
you're a Zen Master
But not by dint
then missing hints
little feat[1] behind the meaning
Blunders mixed
in insights follow.

In some measure,
luckily a Lama's messenger
soothes your temper.
There's some truth in
what was meant
he gently mentions.

Much more seeing in review
maybe now just catching
your intentions then.
Crestfallen
pen scrawls here
sorrow after sorrow.

[1] The band Little Feat.

आर्ष

Seeing you then, knowing clearly
That's not your true self.
Yet astray, even in good works
It's still astray.

आर्ष

You can't give up on me.
I'm not giving up on you.

But if only I was this brave.
If only I could be a Warrior...
Wishing I would play
Like Draymond, Steph and Klay.[1]

Instead, then in hiding
across the Bay, deep in bunkers
Protecting this heart
from the scary darts and mixed up
broken promise-parts, I hunker.

[1] Draymond, Steph and Klay of the The Golden
State Warriors, coached by Steve Kerr, penned
during 2015-2016 season. Go Warriors!

आर्ष

What if I've made a
Terrible mistake?

Will I eat my hat?

Only humility
for our mistakes
saves us now.

Wondering which
hat, how served
will be dinner.

आर्ष

Sometimes dire straits[1]
Resolve an aim
To uncover, making plain
pulling one's own strings[2].
A Lama, beloved, teaches
stealing oneself in Bodhicitta[3]
In Loving Meditation
The Unifying Universe Sings.

[1] The band Dire Straits.
[2] Dyer, Wayne W. *Pulling Your Own Strings*.
   New York: T.Y. Crowell Junior Books, 1978.
   To pioneer and author Wayne Dyer.
[3] The great wish to save sentient beings from
   suffering, helping them to attain or progress on
   the path of awakening.

आर्ष

Primaries, elections kaflooey
Hardly even credible

Citizens utterly unglued
googling countries more tenable.

Where to invade next?[1]
Ahh, Canada.
Is it a wiser society or
a perceptive and endearing
Prime Minister Justin Trudeau?

Trudeau even considers taking up:

>   "how we need poets to
>   change the world"[2]

There's *insight* within--
    Even in his handshake.

Isn't this the wisdom which
draws the many?

---

[1] *Where to Invade Next*. Dir. Michael Moore. 2015.
Michael Moore's record breaking film.
[2] Prime Minister Trudeau to Poet Carolyn Marie
Souaid, 2012, quoted from a letter.

आर्ष

Then I wondered for Pete's sake
What is all this hate[1]?

TV anchor or mind anchor[2]?
That mentality on a screen or
maybe someone near you--
disguised in adult form--
That channel you're
tuned to might be... *is*
teaching you to hate.
Letting their/his thoughts be yours
within and without
Without even a question or a doubt?

Anger is like a virus
destroying from the outside, in.
First it'll take out the joy in
those around you then it'll
shake you down from within.
Shattering all kinds of dreams
you could dream without even
taking them for a spin.
No wonder the great religions
equate it with suffering and sin...

Know that anger & that hate:
that's the path to ruin
No matter how you've thought it out
or considered it to date.

Decide here, decide now
you'll give up this menace &
free yourself of anger and hate[3]--
It's the best chance you'll
have without it: your best chance
to experience love & your true self
--- *letting the sunshine in*[4] ---
no matter what you think of it to date.

[1] Hate or ill-will, includes wishing others ill or
   intending harm or even repetitive negative views
   projected onto others. One example is racism.
[2] Mind anchor: something to which your mind is
   tethered to or to which it repeatedly returns.
[3] To shift from the pain of hate, might require
   receiving empathy.
[4] The 5th Dimension. "Let the Sunshine In." on
   The Age of Aquarius. 1969.
_____ p. 180:_____

[1] Fronsdal, Gil. *The Dhammapada: A New
   Translation of the Buddhist Classic with Annotations.*
   Boston: Shambhala, 2005.
[2] King, Martin Luther. *Strength to Love.* New York:
   Harper & Row, 1963.
[3] Samsara: Sanskrit for suffering in cyclical existence.

आर्ष

Hatred won't cease by hatred[1]
a wisdom Buddha revealed
Darkness won't dispel darkness[2]
A US King appealed.

The entire treasury
all spent for nought.
It's in this cycle of samsara[3] in
which our country's caught.
If instead of a war machine
we built hospitals and schools
we'd not suffer for generations
these thoughts which made us fools.

When we no longer see beings
we label enemies in this worldly scene
then we've won the war for real this time
in this seemingly unceasing warring meme.
Hatred won't stop by hatred
these wisdom beings revealed.
The secret?
It's by love alone.
That's how hatred's healed.

आर्ष

Teach the people love...
Love the people
not with your
high executives pay and
corporate profits before all else:

What about all these unknown
friends, animals & earth itself?

Love the people
not by leading them to hate,
leading them astray,
but lead them to love.
Love them with appreciation, self-worth
love them with jobs &
finding themselves.

As hate while invigorating
is a painful state to those
who know love.

Teach the people love
like Gandhi said it first
by teaching them to throw off their hate.

आर्ष

We humans
are we going to make it
this time?

Are we like our beloved
Polar Bears on their very
last square meter of ice?

The Veneziani[1]
with water
topping top stairs?

Aren't you even a bit surprised
our earth still gives us
her bounty?

Is there no pang of guilt?
What about gratitude for
all these veggies and fruits?
Not even ceasing
neonicotinoids to save
our dear friends the bees?   . . .

[1] Veneziani (ven ettes Zee Ahnee): people
  from Venezia, aka Venice, Italy.

When these shelves are bare
Will we finally honor
the people some call illegal
who kindly break backs to
keep us filled at our table?

Will it then be too late to wake up?
To realize our big mistake?
This movable feast so kindly
tended by life-sustaining
sweat & labors of these fine
Mexican[1] workers and ever ready bees?
Will we then finally see how
inextricably bound we are?

Will you wall out, imprison and poison
these beings who nourish our lives,
our loves and our daily existence?

How, in the end, will you answer to this?

---

[1] While some farmworkers may be US Citizens,
more than half of US farmworkers are
undocumented immigrants. Citizens or not,
the majority of farmworkers are born in Mexico
according to the US Department of Labor.

आर्ष

"They're just taking care of
themselves." The elder emerald
illumined sage's remark dropped in.

आर्ष

Taking heart from a great heart,
the holy one thus named
King of the Jews.
His very being challenging
the existing status quo.

His love so great
From the crucifix
Dying in im/mortal pain, he said,
        Father forgive them
            they know not what they do.

आर्ष

Fannie Lou Townsend Hamer[1]
Amelia Boynton Robinson
Selma[2] Freedom Fighters
Fredrick Douglass[3]
Harriet Tubman[4]
César Chávez[5]
Daisy Bates
Alice Paul
Gandhi
Biko
Jesus
Mandela[6]
Ella Baker[1]
Rosa Parks[7]
Septima Clark[1]
Mohammed Ali
Diane Judith Nash[1]
Dorothy Irene Height[8]
Jo Ann Gibson Robinson[1]
The Reverend Dr. Martin Luther King[9, 10]

Booked or did time. Imprisoned.
Even died for a holy truth.

Involved in nonviolent resistance
Refusing to fight, yet still defending truth.
All, without surrendering their hearts.
Great ones illumined a path of love
with great sacrifice, with compassion
for those they would disprove.

Hallelujah[11]

[1] Olson, Lynne. *Freedom's Daughters : The Unsung Heroines of the Civil Rights Movement from 1830 to 1970.* New York: Scribner, 2001.
[2] *Selma.* Dir. Ava DuVernay. 2014.
[3] Douglass, Frederick. *Narrative of the Life of Frederick Douglass, an American Slave.* Boston: The Anti-Slavery Office, 1845.
[4] Bradford, Sarah. *Harriet Tubman: The Moses of Her People.* Originally published in 1886. Mineola, N.Y.: Dover Publications, Inc., 2004.
[5] *César Chávez: History is Made One Step at a Time.* Dir. Diego Luna. 2014.
[6] Mandela, Nelson. *Long Walk to Freedom: The Autobiography of Nelson Mandela.* Boston: Little, Brown, 1994.
[7] Parks, Rosa, and James Haskins. *Rosa Parks: My Story.* New York: Dial, 1992.
[8] Height, Dorothy. *Open Wide The Freedom Gates: A Memoir.* New York: PublicAffairs, 2005.
[9] King, Martin Luther. *Strength to Love.* New York: Harper & Row, 1963.
[10] So many, many others to include.
[11] Leonard Cohen. "Hallelujah." *Various Positions.* 1984.

आर्ष

Turn your love around[1]
Resolve to see:
heaven and hell
we create right here,
now, in our homes, in our hearts.

See everything as you.
Catch the tip of the thought –
before it creates havoc.
Take a detour to a better notion:
One you might call noisy neighbor...

[1] George Benson. "Turn Your Love Around."
on *Give Me the Night*. 1978.

at least protects me
because they are awake.
This is nonviolence and
saves beings from suffering[1].

Yet you do need sleep
So sleep some sleep tonight.
The suchness of sleep itself
such a profound healer.
Learn to enjoy even this now--
your direct experience.

[1] It's about managing our minds, not about being
silent. It's us we save which then saves myriads
around us. We still, for important reasons, may
want to speak up with wisdom, strength and
skillful means-- even doing this with the many.

आर्ष

Cosmic mind, great mind---

What you have is
buried in thoughts, emotions,
struggles.

Let the contents go and
Celebrate a liberated,
Unsurpassed mind.

आर्ष

"Ataseng!" The Ghanaian
related this greeting.
His face jet dark
blushing in emotion
in recognition of
his mother tongue.

Eyes of mine softened, wet.
Appreciation....

That's all people really want...

आ॒र्ष

Hilarious and ironic.
Comparing fiction with fiction.
Now even Amy and Sheldon's
lives move forward.

　　Even their *snail slow*
　　love affair.

How far behind I feel.
Finding myself here…
Disheartened, in some shock

　　Where did I go wrong?
　　How did I get here?[1]

Last of all
Why am I comparing myself
to Chuck Lorre's characters
from the Big Bang Theory?

How fast the time does go
on this living clock.

[1] Talking Heads, "Once in a Lifetime." on
Remain In Light. 1980.

आर्ष

What happened to the light
Happened to the door.

You see the light
it hadn't worked in years.
Suddenly one day it lit.

    Nonchalantly

Lighting the room as if
nothing happened.
Like it'd been going on
every morning just like that.
Like it was completely *normal*.

आर्ष

Then it happened to the door.
No matter how much
pulling, it wouldn't close.
Yanking it
To no avail
Just days before.
Not just a little ajar--
the door wouldn't even
enter the frame
Not even close.

Then one day
this very door just
slipped into the door frame.
Like magic.

There were no carpenters
No one who'd planed or
shaved, fitting that door.

One day, splendidly
it just came together.
Just like this.

आर्ष

And the day came
when nothing
seemed
impossible.

आर्ष

What is this?
Why is there this
feeling of exhilaration?
The sense that you are
so very close, so near...

आर्षं

Now in Peet's
Beings of light
we call children
swimming their brightly
glowing selves near the window outside.
An aquarium of wonder peering in
Their openness of spirit, fresh
Still filled with love, dazzling the heart
bringing tears to these eyes
touching an exhilaration within.

आर्ष

Lately this remembers
itself from years before

This book you left,
remained behind.

Returning it
at your door
What is it
you silently brandish?

Why it's "What Book!?
Buddha Poems from
Beat to Hiphop"[1].

Innocuously, yes.
It's how you
title waved and vanished.

[1] Gach, Gary. Coyote, Peter. *What Book!?: Buddha Poems from Beat to Hiphop*. Berkeley, CA: Parallax Press, 1998.

आर्ष

Heart as Wide as Open
She gave me
A piece of peace.
The slice of pie
Berry-- what I needed
Superb, unmatched, a high
like from Copper Creek Inn[1].

This was what--
for me?

[1] At the foot of Mount Rainier.

आर्ष

Little creature
Tiniest life perhaps I can see
Crawling across this sunlit page
Love springs forth, a love
Wanting to protect your life.

आर्ष

Mount Rainier
Wildflowers, tender breezes
Enormous luminescent green expanses
Theatre art, in lively rock formations
Trees animated in wind
forming pirouettes
Scintillating light, Mount Rainier
Beloved of the Cascades[1]
How intoxicating in this freeing vortex

[1] Mount Rainier pronounced [rah neer].
Muir called it the noblest.

आर्ष

Leaping faith
revelling in the
unknown-known & unknown

On adventures
Prospering at the
Blue Mountain Source
Mesmerizing awareness

Green, so green
this translucent light
in the forest

आर्ष

In revery
I realized at times
I ran away from you
So afraid of what you say and do

In Shakespeare's play
Even the sorcerer Prospero
Comes to revelation
Realizing the suffering
He's therein proffering.

In a deeper inquiry
I wonder why. *Why?*
Isn't he doing what he wants?

An intuition follows...
This moving away
from destiny brings
its own pain.
Like something's amiss
in the hollows.

आर्ष

Deceived by appearances
A haunted castle
under an unknown spell.

At least, Lumière concedes,
"Whee due hahveh
somme rrezponnezeebilitee fourre
makeeng heem zeh wey hee eez..."[1]

[1] Lumière adapted from *Beauty and the Beast*, Disney
Production, Berkeley Playhouse, Dec. 22, 2016.
Director and Choreographer Kimberly Dooley,
Music Director Eric Walton.
Beauty and the Beast, Music by Alan Menken.
Lyrics by Howard Ashman & Tim Rice. 1993.
Adapted from the screenplay by Linda Woolverton.
Beauty and the Beast. Dir. Gary Trousdale and
Kirk Wise. 1991.
Beauty and the Beast. Dir. Bill Condo, 2017.
Leprince de Beaumont, Jeanne-Marie. *La Belle et la
Bête*. 1748.

आर्ष

"Zhat mey notte beh zeh bezt wey
tue wien zeh gurrl'z affectionnze."[1]

"Hyoue muzt contrrohl yourre tempehrr!"[1]

"Mazterr, whaht ahrre hyoue afrraihd ohv?"[1]

"Hyoue muzt zpeake frromme zeh harrte."[1]

[1] Lumière adapted from *Beauty and the Beast*, Disney
Production, Berkeley Playhouse, Dec. 22, 2016.
Director and Choreographer Kimberly Dooley,
Music Director Eric Walton.
Beauty and the Beast, Music by Alan Menken.
Lyrics by Howard Ashman & Tim Rice. 1993.
Adapted from the screenplay by Linda Woolverton.
Beauty and the Beast. Dir. Gary Trousdale and
Kirk Wise. 1991.
Beauty and the Beast. Dir. Bill Condo, 2017.
Leprince de Beaumont, Jeanne-Marie. *La Belle et la
Bête*. 1748.

आर्ष

Cosmic campground, this earth.
What is this about nature
which brings about such ease?
Flowers, breezes breathe.
No politics with these trees.

Curious is this virtue-power of nature
restoring delight, then laughter
in our inner bees.

आर्ष

How far is it to paradise?
You ask.
Paradise is here
in these trees
in your breathing
Nowhere will you find it
But here.

It just helps to
practice being
in our true nature:

This priceless gem.

आर्ष

These embers
nearly out,
even in grave doubt.
Yet, a feeling remained
deep down below
still glimmering,
there in dim light,
the very last cinder simmering.

आर्ष

Fierce things you said
how could I know...
Their treasures held
deep down below
a fiery dragon's pit
protecting such a diamond.
From a distant peak
viewed from safely
What woe is this?
A truth now here to see--
why it's your vulnerability

_____ p. 208:_____

[1] Wilhelm, Richard, and Cary F. Baynes.
The I Ching: or, Book of Changes. Princeton, NJ:
Princeton University Press, 1967.

आर्ष

Tender realization
like in releasing a spell
another scale off
this dragon fell.
How you are in me
and I am in you.
So states the I Ching's[1]
forty-eighth case:
The town can be moved
but not the well.

आर्ष

You my reader may
be utterly amazed...
Surprised, like a bride
About the dragon
whence delivered from
this untimely spell:
What happens next you wonder
& how do I know
what I do tell.

आर्ष

There's a surprisingly
uplifting lesson from the
riveting Cubs' and Indians'
    2016 World Series.

What is it? You wonder.

Here's how the Cubs
hath spoken:

A 108 year curse
can be broken:
Playing exceedingly skilled ball
Comitting errors along the way &
even *then--* still gallantly
winning the series
rescuing fans and the day.

Yes, making errors is
paradoxically
part of the play--
while still fulfilling
destinies along the way.

आर्ष

Right to the wire
To the very edge of truth
Out of the darkness, anew
We found each other there
Unable, it seems to go
on a moment yonder.

आर्ष

Don't let another day pass—
I can stand it no longer.

Not saying this one truth.

Let the cat out of the bag:
Let it out, the ecstasy and the launder.

आर्ष

Rock Hunter to save his company and for success, spoofs a lover for Rita Marlowe. It's a business stunt to burn Bobo, for ratings.

It's not love. Ultimately, she can't forget George Schmidlap. She's "always trying to turn them into unreasonable facsimiles of George"[1], Vi, her secretary, points out.

"There's nothing between Rita and me. Really there isn't... You know we both owe her a great deal."[1] Rock pleads with Jenny.

"Marrying? Oh, that's just some of Rita's publicity nonsense,"[1] he tells a disbelieving betrothed. "Honey, Rita doesn't love me. She loves a guy named Georgie Schmidlap. She's been trying to forget him, the way I tried to forget you. Only we both failed."[1]

[1] *Will Success Spoil Rock Hunter?* Dir. Frank Tashlin. 1957.

आर्ष

Ah, you remind me: One May day in 14, in the middle of it, eyes on me, you say you love me. In it, your dreams: a honey child-- any kind okay. You want it to happen fast. I want you both two, I want it to last. You say: Throw your hat over the wall and with it our dreams, we'll climb over.

Even if it was you who said you knew all along it would be you and me in the end...

Tonight, I remind you... How the bullet proof vest was put to the test. This brand of kindness just didn't sit, I attest. These friends a pride of lions protecting such a turf-- with everything, all of their worth-- inserting themselves-- clammering, twittering drowning us out-- and all of our earth. As if it was much about them: their opinion first: A decision to be, a decision to birth. Add in much shaming, every trick in the gaming, seriously cheating their training? No one here to blame: It's how the animal kingdom behaves when they are threatened while chasing game. All of this sounds like it's not up to you and me. Any inquiry aside, it's ours to build, see? Teaching that mantra: not to feel guilty. So much presumption, not emotional safety. Guess who convinced you, I didn't love thee? Ethics touted, unreal-- what a strange deal. Do these even feel? Without feedback, all prisoners, sealed. True selves are deceptionless, friendly. Long before a challenge see, a palpable grasp at the palace ici. When such energy abounds, what fun is it to be around? All of this is entirely why I wanted to flee. I get it, to you it's all normal see? When someone doesn't care how you feel, there's no real relationship there to steal. All I can say is maybe I failed miserably.

Now a 180, the town comes a courtin'[1]
There's a recipe for real friendship:
Appreciation, respect, authenticity,
Openness, transparency, trust--
Letting the light shine in on us thus
Receiving feedback, we lean back and listen,
Sharing conscious amends, restorative justice.
Restoring friendship and trust between us.

We only save with kindness within.
Just there, begin.

[1] *The Town That Came A-Courtin'*. Dir. David Winning. 2014.

आर्ष

Remembering such prior actions
Stops the flow of love
Disconnects the heart-love of
Enlightenment
Stops the sunshine mind,
Joy, the rainbow within.

Even the dark
lights the way to the light.

These thoughts-- it's these now within.
What others do--
It's not our true self to cue off of within
Don't nourish your mind with the external
Don't internalize this as being within.

Thus these thinkerings keep us focussed,
Not on our true self, but instead
Away from the light of our own heart within.

May the attention land on the light within,
Remembering, being the sacred heart,
the source, the true being, being within.

आरष

Don't take birth
in any thought.

No tarrying
here or there
like a dragonfly,
no touching down
on a thinking spot.

Instead
land here on this
breath
in this moment
breathing

Practicing this endlessly
Dwell in profound
happiness.
Then save and bless the
whole world with your gifts.

Our whole world needs you.

आर्ष

--- I never knew ---
the universe in Bodhisattvas
protected me
within and without
from who?
It was none other than you.

In the end
Surprising...
Is it possible?
Maybe it was the universe &
You who protected me too--
Protecting the deeper hu[1].

What follows is a journey
with a beloved ever true
The one who loves is within.
And the one I find to love is...
Don't know who: a genuine friend
maybe you or you, or some other--
another honest version of you.

[1] Divine Presence

आर्ष

A night worlds
co-inside:
date night

आर्ष

Pilgrim

Just be here
Speechless
Sitting here in wonder.

We'll get the hang of it.

आर्ष

We talk until dawn
About everything
And you *are* everything.
Still I am nothing.

But underneath your everything
You are nothing and underneath
my nothing, I, too, am everything.

आर्ष

"Did I say I need you?
Did I say I want you?"[1]
Boy, "if I didn't...
I'm a fool you see
No one knows this more than me
As I come clean..."[1]
"Stay with me
You're all I see
"Let's just breathe
"Hold me till I die."[1]

[1] Pearl Jam, "Just Breathe." on *Backspacer*. 2009.

आर्ष

"Give me one good reason
why I should never make a change."[1]
If you want me "then
all of this will go away."[1]

आर्ष

What's different here is he who
listens to me. Now there's someone
here who loves not just *he*
Says and acts like there's no one above me
Happiness true and love abounds through.
His friends wouldn't offend or
without question he would defend me
Our family, the whole world dear, loving others,
it's all very clear: Her beloved dear,
a love reigning with empathy--
true integrity:
It's the universe lavishing
beauty for ashes: aligning love,
truth all at once: with divinity.

[1] George Ezra, "Budapest." on *Wanted on Voyage*. 1980.

आर्ष

Let him gaze upon me
And I upon him.
Do you know how beautiful
you are?

Bewildering you are, really.
Wise & a genius.
Where did you get
that kind of faith?

आर्ष

Don't worry what you'll say
Just Be Here Now[1] in awe

Astonished.
Receiving myriads of kisses
flowing like a stream.

[1] Dass, Ram. . New York: Distributed
by Crown Pub., 1971.

आर्ष

"This is perhaps the greatest risk
any of us will take:

To be seen as we truly are."[1]

"Your Majesty, I'm no princess...
I do not even know if that beautiful
slipper will fit. But, if it does
will you take me as I am?"[1]

"Of course I will. But only if you'll
take me as I am. An apprentice
still learning his trade."[1]

[1] *Cinderella*. Dir. Kenneth Branagh. 2015.
screenplay, Chris Weitz.
Perrault, Charles. *La Petite Pantoufle de Verre*.
1697.

आर्ष

Saving hu[1]
Aligning truth and love.
No other job except being ---
beside the truth infused and okay
an aquarium of wonder--saving beings--
I want.

आर्ष

Unrealistic? Perhaps.
So is the mind of awakening:
Knowing this diamond
mind brings happiness.
Astounding, the wish
to save countless
beings really, isn't it thus?

Even your friend in the
coat of many colors
from a wisdom land
foretold this scores upon
scores of moons ago.

[1] Divine Presence

आर्ष

Celebrating the victory for
all people to marry the one they love[1].

I want this freedom to marry
a beloved clear and trustworthy
the one who loves me so dearly.

आर्ष

All these birds know
their business.
Even the tiniest hummingbirds
& enormous polar bears.

What about us?

[1] Historic US Supreme Court decision on gay
marriage, June 26, 2015, Obergefell v. Hodges.
Such a wonderful gift it is to be happy for and
celebrate the happiness of others.

आर्ष

The grunting caveman
needs this one
for all the unfinished business
in his heart, body and soul.

Grateful
He needs this
Attention badly.

आर्ष

Please
Let me celebrate,
loving all beings
everywhere
I go.

आर्ष

We drank each other's wine
until three in the morning
no wine between us
Spellbound in each other's
Being-presence.

आर्ष

Mecca for friends
Our home
I'll love you in.
Such a little feat[1].

[1] The band Little Feat.

आर्ष

A secret garden
To behold
It's lessons many to unfold
In the light of night
We call day
The universe
She sings us into play.

आर्ष

In the light of the moon
Jupiter conjunct Venus
minting these last words
for a reason.
May it all connect
a lamp for a season
from our hearts
to our zenith

आर्ष

What do poets
do? You ask.

Why by grace or
what seems like luck,
Inspire
a change of art.

The art inside the heArt.

आर्ष

May I and you---
May we and all beings
May we always stay humble and kind[1].
May love
Beyond space and time---
Twinkling in the heart of the universe
Never cease.

[1] Tim McGraw. "Humble and Kind." on
 Damn Country Music. 2015.
 Song written by Lori McKenna.

EPILOGUE

What did those Patriots teach us
most that day?
Is it Tom Brady's
the best quarterback ever to play?
Well, yes maybe and--
What about this?
Never give up the ship and take a dive--
Hidden miracles may be underway.
If you give up now,
you won't see the impossible --
this kind of drive--
to win your own Super Bowl 51
in a historic five[1].

---

[1] The New England Patriot's win over the Atlanta
Falcons was the first overtime win in Super Bowl
history. The Patriots won by erasing a 25 point
Falcon lead, scoring 31 unanswered points.

POSTFACE

Dear Readers,

Thank you for reading. I'm moved by who you are, especially if you read this far.

Rumi said it this way:

> "Lovers don't finally meet somewhere.
> They're in each other all along."[1]

In closing, I'd like to remind you of what Mahatma Gandhi said:

"When I despair, I remember that all through history the ways of truth and love have always won. There have been tyrants, and murderers, and for a time they can seem invincible, but in the end they always fall. Think of it--always."[2]

Just remember, in the end love wins, no matter how long it takes.

[1] Rūmī, Jalāl Al-Dīn, Coleman Barks, and Michael Green. *The Illuminated Rumi*. New York: Broadway, 1997.
[2] Gandhi, Mohandas K., Mahadev H. Desai. *Mohandas K. Gandhi, Autobiography: The Story of My Experiments with Truth*. London: Phoenix Press, 1949.

Now, please go out and create all the love
and magic you can everywhere you go.

"Never give up."[1]
"Just Do It."[2]

I'm praying for you, for all of us.
Wishing you love and many blessings.

Your heart friend,

Muskie
January 8, 2017

PS. Three nights ago in a dream
     I saw you so vividly, so near:
     amazing me, the amazing you.
     Pure magic. "You're a miracle."[3]
     You looked as if you'd been
     humming... in the dream, so it seemed.
     "How am I going to survive a
     lifetime of you surprising me?"[3]

[1] His Holiness the 14th Dalai Lama.
[2] Zen Master Seung Sahn, 1970's, long before Nike.
[3] *Beautiful Creatures*. Dir. Richard LaGravenese.
    2013. Book by Kami Garcia and Margaret Stohl.

Made in the USA
Lexington, KY
06 July 2017